NATIONAL GEOGRAPHIC KiDS

DOGGY DEFENDERS

STELLA

★ ★ ★

THE SEARCH DOG

Lisa M. Gerry

Photographs by Lori Epstein

NATIONAL GEOGRAPHIC
WASHINGTON, D.C.

Meet STELLA!

Stella is a bloodhound. She lives with her family and her best friend, police trooper Enzo Diaz.

Trooper Diaz is also Stella's partner. That's because Stella has a job!

Stella is a search dog. She uses her strong nose to help find people who are lost.

This job is very important. Stella and Trooper Diaz need to practice to stay in tip-top shape.

Today, they are training at the police station.

Trooper Diaz helps Stella get ready by putting on her harness.

To help Stella practice, another trooper hides out of sight. The trooper leaves behind an item that smells like her—a pen!

Stella sniffs the pen.

Sniff, sniff!

Now Stella can track the trooper! Bloodhounds can find people by following the **scents** they leave behind.

This is because bloodhounds have very, very strong noses!

Stella uses her super
nose to follow the
trooper's scent trail.

She's found her! Good job, Stella!

Now that they've practiced, it's time for Stella and Trooper Diaz to patrol. They ride in a special police car.

Stella hops into the back.

Ready to roll!

Suddenly, Trooper Diaz gets
a call on his radio. A hiker has
gone missing, and no one can
find him. Time for Stella to act!

★21★

The hiker got lost in a forest. To get there, Trooper Diaz and Stella will need to ride ... in a helicopter!

Trooper Diaz helps Stella put on her **goggles**.

All set! Stella and Trooper Diaz get into the helicopter and **buckle** in.

It's time for **takeoff.**

What a view!

Stella loves riding in the helicopter.

The helicopter lands where the hiker was last seen. A storm is moving in, and they have to act fast.

Time to get to work!

Luckily, the hiker dropped his bandanna. Stella takes a good sniff.

Sniff, sniff!

She's off!

Stella follows the hiker's scent through the woods, and Trooper Diaz is close behind.

They track the scent
up a fallen log ...

Wait, who is that up ahead? Stella and Trooper Diaz have found the hiker!

Now that he's safe, the happy hiker thanks Stella for rescuing him.

Back at the station, all the troopers thank Stella, too. They are very proud of her: **She saved the day!**

Trooper Diaz is the
proudest of all.
Good dog, Stella!

Meet the Team!

Trooper Diaz answers questions about Stella and being a police trooper.

Q How did you get Stella?

A When I started bloodhound training, Stella and I bonded right away. I officially picked her as my partner after five weeks of school, and we have been together ever since.

Q Who trained Stella?

A I trained Stella initially through a bloodhound school provided by the Virginia Department of Corrections.

Q What do you and Stella do in your free time?

A Stella loves to catch up on her sleep! She also enjoys going on walks with me, my wife Dana, our baby named Fox, and our other dog Dexter.

Dexter

Q **What is Stella's favorite toy?**

A Stella loves to hide bones. She'll spend hours walking around the backyard finding the perfect spot to bury her bone.

Q **What is the best part of being a police trooper?**

A I love the feeling when Stella and I are able to locate a missing person and bring them back home safely to their loved ones. It is extremely rewarding when all that hard work Stella and I put into training pays off.

Stella's Safety Tips

Stella and Trooper Diaz work hard to keep people safe. Here are some ways you can stay safe, too.

1. Know your full name, address, and phone number.

2. Know how and when to dial 911.

3. Don't keep secrets from your parents.

4. Always wear your seat belt.

5. Don't go anywhere with someone you don't know.

6. Don't take anything from strangers.

7. If you get lost indoors (in a mall or store), find the nearest store employee and tell them you are lost and wait there with them.

8. If you get lost outdoors, stay where you are and do not wander off.

Published by National Geographic Partners, LLC. All rights reserved. Reproduction of the whole or any part of the contents without written permission from the publisher is prohibited.

Since 1888, the National Geographic Society has funded more than 12,000 research, exploration, and preservation projects around the world. The Society receives funds from National Geographic Partners, LLC, funded in part by your purchase. A portion of the proceeds from this book supports this vital work. To learn more, visit natgeo.com/info.

NATIONAL GEOGRAPHIC and Yellow Border Design are trademarks of the National Geographic Society, used under license.

For more information, visit nationalgeographic.com, call 1-800-647-5463, or write to the following address:

National Geographic Partners
1145 17th Street N.W.
Washington, D.C. 20036-4688 U.S.A.

Visit us online at nationalgeographic.com/books
For librarians and teachers: ngchildrensbooks.org
More for kids from National Geographic:
natgeokids.com

National Geographic Kids magazine inspires children to explore their world with fun yet educational articles on animals, science, nature, and more. Using fresh story-telling and amazing photography, *Nat Geo Kids* shows kids ages 6 to 14 the fascinating truth about the world—and why they should care.
kids.nationalgeographic.com/subscribe

For information about special discounts for bulk pur-chases, please contact National Geographic Books Special Sales: specialsales@natgeo.com

For rights or permissions inquiries, please contact National Geographic Books Subsidiary Rights: bookrights@natgeo.com

Designed by Callie Broaddus

The publisher would like to thank Lisa Gerry, author; Lori Epstein, photographer; Paige Towler, project editor; Shannon Hibberd, photo editor; and Stella, Trooper Diaz, and the Virginia State Police Aviation Unit, Canine Program, and Fairfax Division for their support and dedication to their communities.

Library of Congress Cataloging-in-Publication Data
Names: Gerry, Lisa, author. | National Geographic Kids (Firm), publisher. | National Geographic Society (U.S.)
Title: Stella the rescue dog / by Lisa M. Gerry.
Description: Washington, DC : National Geographic Kids, [2019] | Series: Doggy defenders | Audience: Ages 4-8. | Audience: K to grade 3.
Identifiers: LCCN 2018031629| ISBN 9781426334498 (hardcover) | ISBN 9781426334504 (hardcover)
Subjects: LCSH: Bloodhound--Juvenile literature. | Search dogs--Juvenile literature. | Rescue dogs--Juvenile literature. | Search and rescue operations--Juvenile literature.
Classification: LCC SF429.B6 G47 2019 | DDC 636.753/6--dc23
LC record available at https://lccn.loc.gov/2018031629

Printed in China
19/PPS/1